Into the Swirl

Charlotte Lit Press
Charlotte Center for Literary Arts, Inc.
PO Box 18607
Charlotte, NC 28218
charlottelit.org/press

Cover art by Lisa Weedman Newell
Author photo by Wendy Yang Brunk

ISBN: 978-1-960558-02-2

PROUD MEMBER

[clmp]

COMMUNITY OF LITERARY MAGAZINES & PRESSES
W W W . C L M P . O R G

Into the Swirl

John Clark

Charlotte Center for Literary Arts, Inc.
Charlotte, North Carolina
charlottelit.org

For my children, Martha, Leslie and Jason,
with my deepest love.

"Man only plays when he is in the fullest sense of the word a human being, and he is only fully a human being when he plays."

—Friedrich Schiller

Contents

Half Circle

I can't name it
a feeling like

the appeal
of a half moon
next to a small cloud

a colt still wet
stretching
to suckle

the threadbare light
painting the lips
of yellow crocus petals

the space between
the tiny open
mouth and thumb
of the exhausted boy
tucked in
on a clear night

the light of stars
from a deep
velvet sky

hum as I trace
the line of your body
beneath the sheet

the rise and fall
of those half-circle curves
catch my breath and carry
me into the spilt
yolk of a new morning

Sleeping with the Moon

I lie in bed in the early morning. The full moon
light streams across the hardwood floor
next to my extended body.
Both body and light are quiet and delicate.

Like lovers following a sweet night's rest.
A night which may have begun with hot
embraces and sweat rides to the edge
of tender touches.

Or truth. Like lovers before sleep
talking about an invitation, disappointment,
the bills, honesty, when to paint
the back room. About time
vanishing. About yearnings.

I am warm in my bed
yet want to lie
on the cold hard floor
in the light. Embrace it.

Believing it is you
all along, that you never
really left, and knowing
my grief at your leaving
will be absorbed by the full moon
just before the birth of the new day sun.

She Becomes a Dream

The undertow of the tide
from the imperial moon
moving in and out
of a sentry of clouds
summons her.

Glass in hand, she surrenders
to the play of her mind
in her bed by the brass-plated lamp.

He is not like the others—
leather sheath with sword
cuts the plane of his narrow hips
his hand in command of the handle

the sun-tinted mail
bordered by the burnt-red
sheen of oriental silk
shields his chest beneath
the craggy rock lookout

wind in his nostrils sings
a lament for her blood
moon scent, his pasty tongue
whips his mouth and lips
for the wetness left
only in his mind.

She stirs and quietly sips
at the edge of her glass
content with this tension
and safe in the sound
of rain on the gray stone patio
outside her open bedroom window.

You Ache

to make coffee. 12 ounces
of water. Exactly. 2 cups
of coffee in a blue-ochre
glazed mug for each
of us. You pour

the clear, fresh water down
and watch it kick back up
and off the walls of the coffee maker
and settle right at the line.
You open

the bag of beans. Precious
deep dark eggs of an ancient
creature who returns
this very morning to deliver
our last hope for eternal life.

The grinder attacks and releases
the smell of dialectics and the irony
of our spending time on TV commentary,
a wraith to the real moments of this morning.

The steam lifts and swirls like words
about our future. About what you need.
About how it all makes sense
like making coffee in the morning. You know

I will not stay. You keep
talking.

Spring Memory

The white pear tree blossoms are bridesmaids
in waiting as spring begins her walk
down the aisle. Lavender willows, heads
bowed, adorn this fertile festival.

Flowers in a passionate profusion
of colors and shapes—pink and white azaleas,
irises and indigos, daffodils and daylilies
reach up and out from the hum of the earth.

Robins in a pair hop in the air
jesters of this pregnant season
of pleasure as it turns to its purpose.

And there by the path
a light blue shell cracked
in two like the love in this season
long ago.

The Conversation at the Next Table

arrives in tangled threads above
fine linens, museum glassware and muted
silver. The flame of the centerpiece candle
skitters here and there in false starts
to flee the wisp of words
of something wrong and wounded.

The conversation of our future marriage
ceases—stopped by the jagged edges
of the nearby voices. Jane and I listen,
look at each other
and long to escape.

Jane is pretty and smart,
optimistic and well-organized.
She will be a good wife and mother
and will secure the future
of her family's reputation.

The conversation at the next table
is over. The middle-aged couple
gone. Jane smiles fearless
in the face of our future. I am stricken
by the vacant seats nearby.

Wanting

You want to please.
You failed you say when
I held back my thunder
to give you ample time
for joy.

I too want to please.
I tell you we are like the bees
in the blossoms of gardenias
beckoning us to dance.

Your hand rises to my shoulder
mine gently settles at your back.

Into the Swirl

Your daring eyes catch me in my silent hut.
They pry me away from a book of alms
and a hard-back chair in the center of a silent room.

Your hair of pure nectar flows into the spirals
of ancient galaxies and wraps around my wounds.
I float up without a thought and fold into the swirl
of your cinnamon sigh.

Your touch is turquoise and my skin stretches
to embrace the whole hue of you. My lips dip
to taste your gift of a honeyed world.

Death appears to be no more than a wraith,
a fallen angel on the ropes as I leave
the gravity of repose. Flowers sing
colors in the new light and trees dance
gigues with the wind.

Listening to Springsteen

sing in the stale quiet
about passion in the streets—
sounds ripping across
my sullen window-picture
of an ordered neighborhood
in a soulless city—a strain
to get on with life
to move through it
waist deep in the mire
of the best that I can do
and frantic about the passion
whose last chord is fading fast

Modernity

You are on ice
in these modern times.

You have a job and friends
and your friends share things
with you and you with them.

Sometimes a friend will call
and say, "Let's go see
some art and have coffee."

You leave your apartment wearing
your favorite beige blouse,
your sandwich made
for tomorrow's lunch,
the cat box cleaned
and your VCR primed
to record the show you know
your friends will see.

You can dance and wear
bright colors. And laugh. Yes—
you can laugh. You know
of the opiate of laughter.

Like life.
A wonderful idea.
A really neat concept.

Alone

The quiet, my partner tonight,
is empty like the vase
after the sunflowers
had rotted and were discarded
leaving

a gaping space like the hunger
for beauty and vibrancy
or simply for a voice
a greeting like the cool
water as it floods the vase
and embraces the fresh-cut stems
of those golden petals.

Freeing the Feminine

Her voice is twisted
and twitching. Bewitching.
And cold. So cold.

And old. Long suffering
the desperate times
of the Phallus.

She clings to the first moon
of the faint light of freedom
to breathe through the frayed
fabric of the Male's mask.

Anima rises tonight from the dank
under-belly of Animus
to dare—

Face me
wrestle me into the fruit
of the dark earth
taste my tongue
the fierce heat of my breath

Hour of the Wolf

Slip behind the eyes of the wolf
as she awakes. Sense the stirring
in your groin move
through sinew and bone
to feel the dew drying
on every single blade of grass
as the sun crests the rolling line
of the hill beyond your den.

Be still.
You are only a breath away
from pure raw drive,
a coupling of fear and hunger
hurtling you into the day's drama.

Know this sacred moment
caught between the ancient
instincts of your kin
and the new light.

Stay with it
and find the sign
of your sudden death
set to strike
just before the stars
take their turn with time.

Carrion Rhapsody

Our bills dip into the rotted
mass of the body, shifting it
with each plunge into syncopated
rhythms—a jazz septet riffing
be-bop notes in the night.

We are clean.
We play the tough parts, digesting
botulism and anthrax—poisons
that would kill you.

Our keen sight leads us through miles
to the delicacy along the well-traveled road.
Our olfactory sense brings bravos
from our feathered brethren.

We know too well the smell
of our reputation among your kind.
Nasty, dirty, disgustingly
ugly.

And the name you have given us—
so close to vulgar
it reeks.

You have seen us in the air.
A soaring symphony on arpeggios of warmth
without moving our wings. You marvel
at our virtuosity in flight.

Yet, you exclaim "Look,
look at that beautiful hawk!"

Existentialist's Ego

Only when willingly
naked will you feel
the raw wind whipping
at your back, the small
hairs along your spine
pinned down and laid back
against the grain of their growing.

Only when weeping
will you reclaim the brine
of your birth. A molting
of hope.

Steel yourself against
the frigid night and you
will break like glass
into pieces too many
to count and too sharp
to cradle.

Seek voices and the company
of comfort and your tongue
will blister and burn.

Confronted by the red eyes
of fear, only you can bring
nature's cool sweet fragility
to your lips and watch as it spills
out into the air like the first
flutter of a newborn bird.

Party Bath

the four-year-old lifts his leg
over the rim and climbs
out of the lion-foot tub—
no towel

heads for the loud talking
in the living room to find Mom
droplets of water
his only wardrobe

rounds the corner
conversation ceases
titters then explosions
of laughter build
as he turns
runs and hides
in the nearest closet

Mom calls for him
throughout the house
as he closes his eyes
and holds his breath
for as long as he can

If We had Met at the Age of 6

You want to climb the tree
and urge me to join you.
Bugs with red backs
are up there you exclaim.
So cool you say.

Sitting in the sand I look at you,
your long spindly legs ending
in sockless pink Keds, head tilting
and almost touching your right shoulder.
I want you to stay.

I've built two mountains with a road
curving around each one. I have a red truck.
I would let you push it around my mountains.

You look at me
and the red truck.
You shrug and walk
toward the tree.

Watching as a Child My Grandmother Die

My body is slight, an accessory after
the frightening fact of her failing.
Frozen, I witness the fall.

It begins slowly. A droplet.
Then two, three—liquid pumped
by the pressure deep inside,
a slow-motion convulsion
of silent logic gently ushering
up the poison from her cankered pain.

It escapes from the left corner
of her mouth. A mouth
of thin lips on a wizened
face. A face of dignity
indifferent to disease.

A drop from her chin stops
time in a free fall.
Then another drop.
And another.

Splayed stains of deep bourbon brown
build at the end of the flow
onto her frayed yellowed
white cotton gown.

Hope for a Moon

I am frightened by the many tiny wrinkles
splayed across my forearm.
Like the rippled sands moving toward the river
I wander in thirst and fear
with so little time before evening.

The pleasant breeze is dying
in a soft light. The chill makes its move
as I hope for a moon to feel by.
A comfort like my grandmother
at her husband's funeral.

Beady eyes in the receiving line
peer from a weave of passing bodies.
Thick words like flawed echoes
off distant cliffs land before her face
but beyond my boyish understanding.

As she leans into my confusion
her wrinkled arm keeps me close
to the rise and fall of her body.
And my breath, like a peach,
hangs easily in the fecund air.

Within a Teardrop is a Story

I arrive at the small park in late afternoon.
A young girl sits on a swing. She's slight
of bearing and unprotected
from the cold by a tattered sweater.

May I help you? I ask. Her lips
move *Yes* and I walk to her.

Her head is bowed and her arms
are wrapped tightly around her thin body.
Her hair, wispy blonde and tangled, dances
in the slight breeze.
She looks up.

There is a tear just below her left eye.
I offer her my long coat and seek
help in the house across the street.

On my return, I see my coat
is crumpled on the ground
by the gently moving empty swing.

I pick it up and from its inside folds
spiraling swirls of golden pixie dust spin
up into the dim sky sending me back
to that tale of the boy who never wanted
to grow up.

Acknowledgements

I must with delight thank the staff of the Charlotte Center for Literary Arts for creating the Chapbook Lab Project and the ten poets with whom I spent a year crafting and critiquing poems. A very special thanks to our monthly mentor poet Dannye Romine Powell—clearly the best teacher of this art form I have had. Appreciation also goes to my quarterly mentor poet Stuart Dischell. Thank you everyone.

About the Author

John Clark writes poems and composes music as a way to play. Professionally, he has been a teacher and nonprofit executive with a 23-year career in public radio. He served as general manager for 18 years at Classical Public Radio WDAV at Davidson College. A native North Carolinian, John holds both undergraduate and masters degrees from University of North Carolina at Chapel Hill. He is the father of three children and two grandchildren. Currently retired, he resides in Charlotte, North Carolina.